EXPERIENCE YOUR GOOD NOW!

EXPERIENCE YOUR GOOD NOW!

Learning to Use Affirmations

Louise Hay

HAY HOUSE, INC.
Carlsbad, California • New York City
London • Sydney • New Delhi

Published in the United States by: Hay House, Inc.: www.hayhouse.com
Published in Australia by: Hay House Australia Pty. Ltd.: www.hayhouse.com.au
Published in the United Kingdom by: Hay House UK, Ltd.: www.hayhouse.co.uk
Published in India by: Hay House Publishers India: www.hayhouse.co.in

Editorial supervision: Jill Kramer • *Design:* Nick C. Welch
Artwork by: Donna Ingemanson, Susy Pilgrim Waters, Anne Smith, Ann Boyajian,
    and Diane Bigda

(Portions of this work have been excerpted from: Louise Hay's *Power Thought* card deck;
the book/CD *"I Can Do It®,"* and the books *You Can Heal Your Life* and the *You Can Heal
Your Life Companion Book*—all published by Hay House.)

Library of Congress Control No.: 2009937001

Tradepaper ISBN: 978-1-4019-4706-4
E-book ISBN: 978-1-4019-2849-0

1st edition, May 2010

Printed in the United States of America

Contents

*"Affirmations are like planting seeds in the ground. First they germinate, then they sprout roots, and then they shoot up through the ground. It takes some time to go from a seed to a full-grown plant. And so it is with affirmations—it takes some time from the first declaration to the final demonstration.
Be patient."*

— Louise Hay

CHAPTER 1

Introduction

Welcome to the world of affirmations. By choosing to use the tools in this book, you've made a conscious decision to heal your life and move forward on the path of positive change . . . and the time for that positive change is now! There is no time like the present for you to take control of your thoughts. Join the countless numbers of people who have changed their lives for the better by doing what I'm going to suggest to you in these pages.

Doing affirmations is not hard work. It can be a joyous experience as you lift the burden of old negative beliefs and release them back to the nothingness from whence they came.

Just because we've believed something negative about ourselves or about our lives does not mean that there is any truth to it. As children, we hear negative things about ourselves and about life and we accept these ideas as if they're true. Now, we're going to examine the things we've believed and make a decision to either continue to believe them because they support us and make our life joyful and fulfilled, or make the decision to release them. I like to imagine that I'm letting go of old beliefs by dropping them into a river, and they gently drift downstream and dissolve and disappear, never to return again.

Come into my garden of life and plant new thoughts and ideas that are beautiful and nourishing. Life loves you and wants you to have the very best. Life wants you to have peace of mind, inner joy, confidence, and an abundance of self-worth and self-love. You deserve to feel at ease at all times with all people and to earn a good living. So let me help you plant these ideas in your new garden. You can nourish them and watch them grow into beautiful flowers and fruits that will in turn feed and nourish you all of your life.

On the accompanying audio download, I offer you more helpful information about affirmations that you can apply to virtually every aspect of your life. (Download instructions and track list are at the end of this book.) Feel free to listen to it at any time of the day or night—whenever you'd like positive thoughts and ideas to permeate your consciousness and fill you with hope and joy.

CHAPTER 2

What Are Affirmations?

For those of you who aren't familiar with affirmations and have never worked with them, I'd like to explain a little about what they are and how they work. Very simply, an affirmation is anything you say or think. A lot of what people normally say and think is quite negative and doesn't create good experiences. You have to retrain your thinking and speaking into positive patterns if you want to heal your life.

An affirmation opens the door. It's a beginning point on the path to change. In essence, you're saying to your subconscious mind: *"I am taking responsibility. I am aware that there is something I can do to change."* When I talk about *doing affirmations*, I mean consciously choosing words that will either help *eliminate* something from your life or help *create* something new in your life.

Every thought you think and every word you speak is an affirmation. All of your self-talk, your internal dialogue, is a stream of affirmations. You're using affirmations every moment whether you know it or not. You're affirming and creating your life experiences with every word and thought.

Your beliefs are merely habitual thinking patterns that you learned as a child. Many of them work very well for you. Other beliefs may be limiting your ability to create the very things you say you want. What you want and what you believe you deserve may be very different. You need to pay attention to your thoughts so that you can begin to eliminate the ones creating experiences you do *not* want in your life.

Please realize that every complaint is an affirmation of something you think you don't want in your life. Every time you get angry, you're affirming that you want more anger in your life. Every time you feel like a victim, you're affirming that you want to *continue* to feel like a victim. If you feel that Life isn't giving you what you want, then it's certain that you will never have the goodies that Life gives to others—that is, until you change the way you think and talk.

You're not a bad person for thinking the way you do. You've just never learned *how* to think and talk. People throughout the world are just now beginning to learn that thoughts create experiences. Your parents probably didn't know this, so they couldn't possibly teach it to you. They taught you how to look at life in the way that *their* parents taught them. So nobody is *wrong*. However, it's time for you to wake up and begin to consciously create your life in a way that pleases and supports you. *You* can do it. *I* can do it. *We all* can do it—we just need to learn how. So let's get to it.

Throughout this book, I'll talk about specific topics and concerns (health, fearful emotions, critical thinking, addictions, forgiveness, work, money and prosperity, friends, love and intimacy, and aging) and give you exercises that will show you how to make positive changes in these areas.

Some people say that "affirmations don't work" (which is an affirmation in itself), when what they mean is that they don't know how to use them correctly. They may say, *"My prosperity is growing,"* but then think, *Oh, this is stupid, I know it won't work.* Which affirmation do you think will win out? The negative one, of course, because it's part of a long-standing, habitual way of looking at life. Sometimes people will say their affirmations once a day and complain the rest of the time. It will take a long time for affirmations to work if they're done that way. The complaining affirmations will always win, because there are more of them, and they're usually said with great feeling.

However, *saying* affirmations is only part of the process. What you do the rest of the day and night is even more important. The secret to having your affirmations work quickly and consistently is to prepare an atmosphere in which they can grow. Affirmations are like seeds planted in soil. Poor soil, poor growth. Rich soil, abundant growth. The more you choose thoughts that make you feel good, the quicker the affirmations work.

So think happy thoughts. It's that simple. And it *is* doable. The way you choose to think, right now, is just that—a choice. You may not realize it because you've thought this way for so long, but it really is a choice.

Now . . . today . . . this moment . . . you can choose to change your thinking. Your life won't turn around overnight, but if you're consistent and make the choice on a daily basis to think thoughts that make you feel good, you'll definitely make positive changes in every area of your life.

Creating Affirmations

Doing affirmations is consciously choosing to think certain thoughts that will manifest positive results in the future. They create a focal point that will allow you to begin changing your thinking. Affirmative statements are *going beyond the reality of the present into the creation of the future through the words you use in the now.*

When you choose to say *"I am very prosperous,"* you may actually have very little money in the bank at the moment, but what you're doing is planting seeds for future prosperity. Each time you repeat this statement, you're reaffirming the seeds you've planted in the atmosphere of your mind. That's why you want it to be a *happy* atmosphere. Things grow much quicker in fertile, rich soil.

It's important for you to always say your affirmations in the *present* tense, and without contractions. (Although I use contractions throughout the running text of my books, I never use them in affirmations, since I don't want to diminish their power.) For example, typical affirmations would start: *"I have . . ."* or *"I am . . ."* If you say, "I am going to . . ." or "I will have . . . ," then your thought stays out there in the future. The Universe takes your thoughts and words very literally and gives you what you say you want. *Always.* This is another reason to maintain a happy mental atmosphere. It's easier to think in positive affirmations when you feel good.

Think of it this way: Every thought you think counts, so don't waste your precious thoughts. Every positive thought brings good into your life. Every negative thought pushes good away; it keeps it just out of your reach. How many times in your life have you almost gotten something good and it seemed to be snatched away at the last moment? If you could remember what your mental atmosphere was like at those times, you'd have the answer. Too many negative thoughts create a barrier against positive affirmations.

If you say, "I don't want to be sick anymore," this is not an affirmation for good health. You have to state clearly what you *do* want: *"I accept perfect health now."* "I hate this car" does not bring you a wonderful new car because you're not being clear. Even if you do get a new car, in a short time you'll probably hate it, because that's what you've been affirming. If you want a new car, then say something like this: *"I have a beautiful new car that suits all of my needs."*

You'll hear some people saying, "Life sucks!" (which is a terrible affirmation). Can you imagine what experiences *that* statement will attract to you? Of course, it isn't life that sucks, it's your *thinking* that sucks. That thought will help you feel terrible. And when you feel terrible, no good can come into your life.

Don't waste time arguing for your limitations: poor relationships, problems, illnesses, poverty, and so on. The more you talk about the problem, the more you anchor it in place. Don't blame others for what is seemingly wrong in your life—that's just another waste of time. Remember, you're under the laws of your own consciousness, your own thoughts, and you attract specific experiences to you as a result of the way you think.

Now, let's deal with some specific topics.

※-※※-※

Author's note: All exercises in the chapters that follow need to be done on a separate piece of paper, so I recommend that you keep a pad of paper or a blank journal handy as you use this book.

CHAPTER 3

Affirmations for Health

"I restore and maintain my body at optimal health."

Health Checklist

Check the items below that you believe are applicable to you. By the end of this chapter, you'll be able to counter these negative thoughts with positive ones.

- ❏ I get three colds every year.
- ❏ My energy level is low.
- ❏ I heal slowly.
- ❏ My allergies act up constantly.
- ❏ Heart dis-ease runs in my family.
- ❏ I get one illness after another.
- ❏ My back gives me constant pain.
- ❏ These headaches never go away.
- ❏ I'm always constipated.
- ❏ I have sore feet.
- ❏ I'm constantly hurting my body.

Be very clear that your body is *always* trying to maintain a state of optimal health, no matter how badly you treat it. If you take good care of your body, it will reward you with vibrant health and energy.

I believe that we contribute to every "illness" in our body. The body, as with everything else in life, is a mirror of our inner thoughts and beliefs. Our body is always talking to us, if we will only take the time to listen. Every cell within our bodies responds to every single thought we think.

When we discover what the mental pattern is behind an illness, we have a chance to change the pattern and, therefore, the dis-ease. Most people don't want to be sick on a conscious level, yet every dis-ease that we have is a teacher. Illness is the body's way of telling us that there's a false idea in our consciousness. Something that we're believing, saying, doing, or thinking is not for our highest good. I always picture the body tugging at us saying, "Please—pay attention!"

Sometimes people *do* want to be sick. In our society, we've made illness a legitimate way to avoid responsibility or unpleasant situations. If we can't learn to say no, then we may have to invent a dis-ease to say no for us.

I read an interesting report a few years back. It stated that only 30 percent of patients follow their doctor's instructions. According to Dr. John Harrison, author of the fascinating book *Love Your Disease,* many people go to doctors only to have their acute symptoms relieved—so that they can *tolerate* their dis-ease. It's as if an unwritten, subconscious agreement exists between doctor and patient: The doctor agrees not to cure the patient if the patient pretends to do something about his or her condition.

Also in this agreement, one person gets to pay, and the other becomes the authority figure . . . and so, both parties are satisfied.

True healing involves body, mind, and spirit. I believe that if we "cure" an illness yet do not address the emotional and spiritual issues that surround that ailment, it will only manifest again.

EXERCISE: Releasing Your Health Problems

Are you willing to release the need that has contributed to your health problems? Once again, when you have a condition that you want to change, the first thing that you have to do is say so. Say: *"I am willing to release the need in me that has created this condition."* Say it again. Say it looking in the mirror. Say it every time you think about your condition. It's the first step in creating a change. Now, do the following:

1. List all of your mother's illnesses.
2. List all of your father's illnesses.
3. List all of *your* illnesses.
4. Do you see a connection?

EXERCISE: Health and Dis-ease

Let's examine some of your beliefs about health and dis-ease. Answer the following questions. Be as open and honest as you can.

1. What do you remember about your childhood illnesses?
2. What did you learn from your parents about illness?
3. What, if anything, did you enjoy about being sick as a child?
4. Is there a belief about illness from your childhood that you're still acting on today?
5. How have you contributed to the state of your health?
6. Would you like your health to change? If so, in what way?

EXERCISE: Your Beliefs about Sickness

Complete the following statements as honestly as you can.

1. The way I make myself sick is . . .
2. I get sick when I try to avoid . . .
3. When I get sick, I always want to . . .
4. When I was sick as a child, my mother always . . .
5. My greatest fear when I'm sick is that . . .

EXERCISE: The Power of Affirmations

Let's discover the power of written affirmations! Writing an affirmation can intensify its power. Write a positive affirmation about your health 25 times. You may create your own, or use one of the following:

My healing is already in process.
I listen with love to my body's messages.
My health is radiant, vibrant, and dynamic now.
I am grateful for my perfect health.
I deserve good health.

EXERCISE: Self-Worth

Let's examine the issue of self-worth with respect to your health. Answer the following questions, then create a positive affirmation to counter each one if your response was a negative one.

1. Do I deserve good health?

    Sample Answer: *No. Illness runs in my family.*
    Sample Affirmation: *I accept and deserve perfect health now.*

2. What do I fear most about my health?

    Sample Answer: *I'm afraid that I'll get sick and die.*
    Sample Affirmation: *It is safe to be well now. I am always loved.*

3. What am I "getting" from this belief?

    Sample Answer: *I don't have to be responsible or go to work.*
    Sample Affirmation: *I am confident and secure. Life is easy for me.*

4. What do I fear will happen if I let go of this belief?

> **Sample Answer:** *I'll have to grow up.*
> **Sample Affirmation:** *It is safe for me to be an adult.*

The statements in the checklist at the beginning of this chapter are repeated below, along with an affirmation corresponding to each belief. Make these affirmations part of your daily routine. Say them often in the car, at work, while looking in the mirror, or anytime you feel your negative beliefs surfacing.

I get three colds every year.
I am safe and secure at all times. Love surrounds me and protects me.

My energy level is low.
I am filled with energy and enthusiasm.

I heal slowly.
My body heals rapidly.

My allergies act up constantly.
My world is safe. I am safe. I am at peace with all of Life.

Heart dis-ease runs in my family.
I am not my parents. I am healthy and whole and filled with joy.

I get one illness after another.
Good health is mine now. I release the past.

My back gives me constant pain.
Life loves and supports me. I am safe.

These headaches never go away.
I no longer criticize myself; my mind is at peace, and all is well.

I'm always constipated.
I allow life to flow through me.

I have sore feet.
I am willing to move forward with ease.

I'm always hurting my body.
I am gentle with my body. I love myself.

"I give myself permission to be well."

Health Treatment

I am one with Life, and all of Life loves me and supports me. Therefore, I claim for myself perfect, vibrant health at all times. My body knows how to be healthy, and I cooperate by feeding it healthy foods and beverages, and exercising in ways that are enjoyable to me. My body loves me, and I love and cherish my precious body. I am not my parents, nor do I choose to re-create their illnesses. I am my own unique self; and I move through life healthy, happy, and whole. This is the truth of my being, and I accept it as so. All is well in my body.

CHAPTER 4

Affirmations for Fearful Emotions

"Fears are merely thoughts, and thoughts can be released."

Fearful Emotions Checklist

Check the items below that you believe are applicable to you. By the end of this chapter, you'll be able to counter these negative thoughts with positive ones.

- ❏ I'm anxious all the time.
- ❏ Nothing works for me.
- ❏ Growing older frightens me.
- ❏ I'm afraid of flying.
- ❏ People scare me.
- ❏ What if I become homeless?
- ❏ I have difficulty expressing my feelings.
- ❏ My temper is out of control.
- ❏ I can't focus on anything.
- ❏ Everyone is against me.
- ❏ I feel like a failure.

❑   What if I have to endure a painful death?
❑   I'm scared of being alone.

In any given situation, I believe that we have a choice between love and fear. We experience fear of change, fear of not changing, fear of the future, and fear of taking a chance. We fear intimacy, and we fear being alone. We fear letting people know what we need and who we are, and we fear letting go of the past.

At the other end of the spectrum, we have love. Love is the miracle we're all looking for. Loving ourselves works miracles in our lives. I'm not talking about vanity or arrogance, because that's not love. That's fear. I'm talking about having great respect for ourselves, and gratitude for the miracle of our body and mind.

Remind yourself when you're frightened that you're not loving and trusting yourself. Not feeling "good enough" interferes with the decision-making process. How can you make a good decision when you're not sure about yourself?

Susan Jeffers, in her marvelous book *Feel the Fear and Do It Anyway,* states that "if everybody feels fear when approaching something totally new in life, yet so many are out there 'doing it' despite the fear, then we must conclude that *fear is not the problem.*" She goes on to say that the real issue is not the fear, but how we *hold* the fear. We can approach it from a position of power or a position of helplessness. The fact that we have the fear becomes irrelevant.

We see what we *think* the problem is, and then we find out what the *real* problem is. Not feeling "good enough" and lacking self-love are the real problems.

Emotional problems are among the most painful of all. Occasionally we may feel angry, sad, lonely, guilty, anxious, or frightened. When these feelings take over and become predominant, our lives can become emotional battlegrounds.

What we *do* with our feelings is important. Are we going to act out in some way? Will we punish others or force our will upon them? Will we somehow abuse ourselves?

The belief that we're *not good enough* is often at the root of these problems. Good mental health begins with *loving the self*. When we love and approve of ourselves *completely*—the good and the so-called bad—we can begin to change.

Part of self-acceptance is releasing other people's opinions. Many of the things we've chosen to believe about ourselves have absolutely no basis in truth.

For example, a young man named Eric was a client of mine several years ago when I was seeing people privately. He was devastatingly handsome and made a good living as a model. He told me how difficult it was for him to go to the gym because he felt so unattractive.

As we worked together, he recalled that a neighborhood bully from his childhood used to call him "ugly." This person would also beat him up and constantly threaten him. In order to be left alone and feel safe, Eric began to hide. He bought into the idea that he wasn't good enough. In his mind, he *was* ugly.

Through self-love and doing positive affirmations, Eric has improved tremendously. His feelings of anxiety may come and go, but now he has some tools to work with.

Remember, feelings of inadequacy start with negative thoughts that we have about ourselves. However, these thoughts have no power over us unless we act upon them. Thoughts are only words strung together. They have *no meaning whatsoever.* Only *we* give meaning to them, and we do so by focusing on the negative messages over and over again in our minds. We believe the worst about ourselves. And *we* choose what *kind* of meaning we give to them.

We're always perfect, always beautiful, and ever-changing. We're doing the best we can with the understanding, knowledge, and awareness we have. As we grow and change more and more, our "best" will only get better and better.

EXERCISE: Letting Go

As you read this exercise, take a deep breath, and as you exhale, allow the tension to leave your body. Let your scalp, forehead, and face relax. Your head need not be tense in order for you to read. Let your tongue, throat, and shoulders relax. Let your back, abdomen, and pelvis relax. Let your breathing be at peace as you relax your legs and feet.

Can you feel a noticeable change in your body since you started reading the previous paragraph? In this relaxed, comfortable position, say to yourself, *"I am willing to let go. I release. I let go. I release all tension. I release all fear. I release all anger. I release all guilt. I release all sadness. I let go of old limitations. I let go, and I am at peace. I am at peace with myself. I am at peace with the process of life. I am safe."*

Go over this exercise two or three times. Repeat it whenever thoughts of difficulty come up. It takes a little practice for the routine to become a part of you. Once you're familiar with this exercise, you can do it anywhere at any time. You will be able to relax completely in any situation.

EXERCISE: Fears and Affirmations

After each category listed below, write down your greatest fear. Then, think of a positive affirmation that would correspond to it.

1. **CAREER**

    Sample Fear: *I'm afraid that no one will ever see my value.*
    Sample Affirmation: *Everybody at work appreciates me.*

2. **LIVING SITUATION**

    Sample Fear: *I'll never have a place of my own.*
    Sample Affirmation: *There is a perfect home for me, and I accept it now.*

3. **FAMILY RELATIONS**

    Sample Fear: *My parents won't accept me the way I am.*
    Sample Affirmation: *I accept my parents, and they, in turn, accept and love me.*

4. **MONEY**

> **Sample Fear:** *I'm afraid of being poor.*
> **Sample Affirmation:** *I trust that all my needs will be taken care of.*

5. **PHYSICAL APPEARANCE**

> **Sample Fear:** *I think I'm fat and unattractive.*
> **Sample Affirmation:** *I release the need to criticize my body.*

6. **SEX**

> **Sample Fear:** *I'm afraid that I'll have to "perform."*
> **Sample Affirmation:** *I am relaxed, and I flow with life easily and effortlessly.*

7. **HEALTH**

> **Sample Fear:** *I'm afraid I'll get sick and won't be able to take care of myself.*
> **Sample Affirmation:** *I always attract all the help I need.*

8. **RELATIONSHIPS**

> **Sample Fear:** *I don't think anyone will ever love me.*
> **Sample Affirmation:** *Love and acceptance are mine. I love myself.*

9.   OLD AGE

Sample Fear: *I'm afraid of getting old.*
Sample Affirmation: *Every age has its infinite possibilities.*

10.   DEATH AND DYING

Sample Fear: *What if there's no life after death?*
Sample Affirmation: *I trust the process of life. I am on an endless journey through eternity.*

EXERCISE: Positive Affirmations

Choose an area of fear from the last exercise that's most pertinent and pressing for you. Using visualization, see yourself going through the fear with a positive outcome. See yourself feeling free and being at peace.

Now write down a positive affirmation 25 times. Remember the power you're tapping into!

EXERCISE: Have Fun with Your Inner Child

When you're in a state of anxiety or fear that keeps you from functioning, you may have abandoned your inner child. Think of some ways in which you can reconnect with your inner child. What could you do for fun? What could you do that is *just for you?*

List 15 ways in which you could have fun with your inner child. You may enjoy reading good books, going to the movies, gardening, keeping a journal, or taking a hot bath. How about some "child-like" activities? Really take the time to think. You could run on the beach, go to a playground and swing on a swing, draw pictures with crayons, or climb a tree. Once you've made your list, try at least one activity each day. Let the healing begin!

Look at all you've discovered! Keep going—you can create such fun for you and your inner child! Feel the relationship between the two of you healing.

The statements in the checklist at the beginning of this chapter are repeated below, along with an affirmation corresponding to each belief. Make these affirmations part of your daily routine. Say them often in the car, at work, while looking in the mirror, or anytime you feel your negative beliefs surfacing.

I'm anxious all the time.
I am at peace.

Nothing works for me.
My decisions are always perfect for me.

Growing older frightens me.
My age is perfect, and I enjoy each new moment.

I'm afraid of flying.
I center myself in safety and accept the perfection of my life.

People scare me.
I am loved and safe wherever I go.

What if I become homeless?
I am at home in the Universe.

I have difficulty expressing my feelings.
It is safe for me to express my feelings.

My temper is out of control.
I am at peace with myself and my life.

I can't focus on anything.
My inner vision is clear and unclouded.

Everyone is against me.
I am lovable, and everybody appreciates me.

I feel like a failure.
My life is a success.

What if I have to endure a painful death?
I die peacefully and comfortably at the right time.

I'm scared of being alone.
I express love, and I always attract love wherever I go.

"I give myself permission to be at peace."

Feeling-Good Treatment

I am one with Life, and all of Life loves and supports me. Therefore, I claim for myself emotional well-being at all times. I am my best friend, and I enjoy living with myself. Experiences come and go, and people come and go, but I am always here for myself. I am not my parents, nor their patterns of emotional unhappiness. I choose to think only thoughts that are peaceful, joyous, and uplifting. I am my own unique self; and I move through life in a comfortable, safe, and peaceful way. This is the truth of my being, and I accept it as so. All is well in my heart and my mind.

CHAPTER 5

Affirmations for Critical Thinking

"I accept all my emotions, but choose not to wallow in them."

Critical-Thinking Checklist

Check the items below that you believe are applicable to you. By the end of this chapter, you'll be able to counter these negative thoughts with positive ones.

- ❑ People are so stupid.
- ❑ I'd do it if I weren't so fat.
- ❑ Those are the ugliest clothes I've ever seen.
- ❑ They'll never be able to finish the job.
- ❑ I'm such a klutz.
- ❑ If I get angry, I'll lose control.
- ❑ I have no right to be angry.
- ❑ Anger is bad.
- ❑ When someone is angry, I get scared.
- ❑ It's not safe to be angry.
- ❑ I won't be loved if I get mad.

❏ Stuffing anger makes me sick.
❏ I've never been angry.
❏ My neighbors are so noisy.
❏ Nobody asks me what I think.

Does your internal dialogue sound like this? Is your inner voice constantly picking, picking, picking? Are you seeing the world through critical eyes? Do you judge everything? Do you stand in self-righteousness?

Most of us have such a strong tendency to judge and criticize that we can't easily break the habit. However, it's the most important issue to work on immediately. We'll never be able to really love ourselves until we go beyond the need to make life wrong.

As a little baby, you were so open to life. You looked at the world with eyes of wonder. Unless something was scary or someone harmed you, you accepted life just as it was. Later, as you grew up, you began to accept the opinions of others and make them your own.

You learned how to criticize.

EXERCISE: Letting Go of Critical Thinking

Let's examine some of your beliefs about critical thinking. Answer the following questions. Be as open and honest as you can.

1. What was your family pattern?
2. What did you learn about criticism from your mother?

3. What were the things she criticized?

4. Did she criticize you? If so, for what?

5. When was your father judgmental?

6. Did he judge himself?

7. How did your father judge you?

8. Was it a family pattern to criticize each other? If so, how and when did your family members do so?

9. When is the first time you remember being criticized?

10. How did your family judge your neighbors?

Now answer the following questions:

• Did you have loving, supportive teachers at school, or were they always telling you what was lacking in you? What sort of things *did* they tell you?

• Can you begin to see where you might have picked up a pattern of being critical? Who was the most critical person in your childhood?

I believe that criticism shrivels our spirits. It only reinforces the belief that we're "not good enough." It certainly doesn't bring out the best in us.

EXERCISE: Replacing Your "Shoulds"

As I've said many times, I believe that *should* is one of the most damaging words in our language. Every time we use it, we are, in effect, saying that we *are* wrong, or we *were* wrong, or we're *going to be* wrong. I would like to take the word *should* out of our vocabulary forever, and replace it with the word *could*. This word gives us a choice, and then we're never wrong.

Think of five things that you "should" do. Then replace *should* with *could*.

Now, ask yourself, *"Why haven't I?"* You may find that you've been berating yourself for years for something that you never wanted to do in the first place, or for something that was never your idea. How many "shoulds" can you drop from your list?

EXERCISE: My Critical Self

Criticism breaks down the inner spirit and never changes a thing. Praise builds up the spirit and can bring about positive change. Write down two ways in which you criticize yourself in the area of love and intimacy. Perhaps you're not able to tell people how you feel or what you need. Maybe you have a fear of relationships, or you attract partners who will hurt you. Then, think of something you can praise yourself for in this area.

Examples:

I criticize myself for: *choosing people who aren't able to give me what I need, and for being clingy in relationships.*

I praise myself for: *being able to tell someone that I like him/her (it scared me, yet I did it anyway); and for allowing myself to be openly loving and affectionate.*

Now think of things you criticize yourself for and ways you can praise yourself in those areas.

Congratulations! You've just begun to break another old habit! You're learning to praise yourself—in this moment. And the point of power is *always* in the present moment.

EXERCISE: Acknowledging Our Feelings

Anger is a natural and normal emotion. Babies get furious, express their fury, and then it's over. Many of us have learned that it's not nice, polite, or acceptable to be angry. We learn to swallow our angry feelings. They settle in our bodies, in the joints and muscles, and then they accumulate and become resentment. Layer upon layer of buried anger turned into resentment can contribute to dis-eases such as arthritis, assorted aches and pains, and even cancer.

We need to acknowledge all our emotions, including anger, and find positive ways to express these feelings. We don't have to hit people or dump on them, yet we can say simply and clearly, "This makes me angry," or "I'm angry about what you did." If it's not appropriate to say this, we still have many options: We can scream into a pillow, hit a punching bag, run, yell in the car with the windows rolled up, play tennis, or any number of other things. These are all healthy outlets.

1. What was the pattern of anger in your family?

2. What did your father do with his anger?

3. What did your mother do with her anger?

4. What did your brothers or sisters do with their anger?

5. Was there a family scapegoat?

6. What did *you* do with your anger as a child?

7. Did you express your anger, or did you stuff it?

8. What method did you use to hold it in?

9. Were you . . .

. . . an overeater?	Yes	No
. . . always sick?	Yes	No
. . . accident prone?	Yes	No
. . . getting into fights?	Yes	No
. . . a poor student?	Yes	No
. . . crying all of the time?	Yes	No

10. How do you handle your anger now?

11. Do you see a family pattern?

12. Which family member are you like when it comes to expressing anger?

13. Do you have a "right" to be angry?

14. Why or why not? Who said so?

15. Can you give yourself permission to express all your feelings in appropriate ways?

In order for a child to grow and blossom, he or she needs love, acceptance, and praise. We can be shown "better" ways to do things without making the way we do it "wrong." The child within you still needs that love and approval.

You can say the following positive statements to your inner child:

"I love you and know that you're doing the best you can."

"You're perfect just as you are."

"You become more wonderful every day."

"I approve of you."

"Let's see if we can find a better way to do this."

"Growing and changing is fun, and we can do it together."

These are words that children want to hear. It makes them feel good. When they feel good, they do their best. They unfold beautifully.

If your child, or your inner child, is used to constantly being "wrong," it may take a while for him or her to accept the new, positive words. If you make a definite decision to release criticism and you're consistent, you can work miracles.

Give yourself one month to talk to your inner child in positive ways. Use the affirmations listed above, or make up a list of your own. Carry a list of these affirmations with you. When you notice yourself becoming judgmental, take out the list and read it two or three times. Better yet, speak it aloud in front of a mirror.

EXERCISE: Listen to Yourself

This exercise requires a tape recorder. Tape your telephone conversations for a week or so—just your voice. When the tape is filled on both sides, sit down and listen to it. Listen to not only what you say, but the way you say it. What are your beliefs? Who and what do you criticize? Which parent, if any, do you sound like?

As you release the need to pick on yourself all the time, you'll notice that you no longer criticize others so much. When you make it okay to be yourself, then you automatically allow others to be themselves. Their little habits no longer bother you so much. You release the need to change them. As you stop judging *others,* they release the need to judge *you.* Everybody wants to be free.

You may be a person who criticizes everyone around you. And if you do, you will certainly criticize yourself, too. So you may ask yourself:

1. What do I get from being angry all the time?
2. What happens if I let go of my anger?
3. Am I willing to forgive and be free?

EXERCISE: Write a Letter

Think of someone you're angry with. Perhaps it's an old anger. Write this person a letter. Tell him or her all your grievances and how you feel. Don't hold back. Really express yourself. When you've finished the letter, read it once, then fold it, and on the outside write: "What I really want is your love and approval." Then burn the letter and release it.

Mirror Work

Mirror work is simple and very powerful. It simply involves looking into a mirror when you say your affirmations. Mirrors reflect your true feelings back to you. As children, you received most of your negative messages from adults, many of them looking you straight in the eye and perhaps even shaking a finger at you.

Today, when most of us look into a mirror, we'll say something negative. We either criticize our looks, or berate ourselves for something else.

To look yourself in the eye and make a positive declaration is one of the quickest ways to get positive results with affirmations. I ask people to look in their eyes and say something positive about themselves every time they pass a mirror.

So, right now, think of another person, or even the same person once again, whom you're angry with. Sit down in front of a mirror. Be sure to have some tissues nearby. Look into your own eyes and "see" the other person. Tell this person what you're so angry about.

When you're finished, tell him or her, "What I really want is your love and approval." We're all seeking love and approval. That's what we want from everyone, and that's what everyone wants from us. Love and approval bring harmony into our lives.

In order to be free, you need to release the old ties that bind you. So once again, look into the mirror and affirm to yourself, *"I am willing to release the need to be an angry person."* Notice if you're really willing to let go, or if you're holding on to the past.

❤

The statements in the checklist at the beginning of this chapter are repeated below, along with an affirmation corresponding to each belief. Make these affirmations part of your daily routine. Say them often in the car, at work, while looking in the mirror, or anytime you feel your negative beliefs surfacing.

People are so stupid.
Everybody is doing the best they can, including me.

I'd do it if I weren't so fat.
I appreciate the wonder of my body.

Those are the ugliest clothes I've ever seen.
I love the uniqueness that people express in their clothing.

They'll never be able to finish the job.
I release the need to criticize others.

I'm such a klutz.
I become more proficient every day.

If I get angry, I'll lose control.
I express my anger in appropriate places and ways.

I have no right to be angry.
All of my emotions are acceptable.

Anger is bad.
Anger is normal and natural.

When someone is angry, I get scared.
I comfort my inner child, and we are safe.

It's not safe to be angry.
I am safe with all of my emotions.

I won't be loved if I get mad.
The more honest I am, the more I am loved.

Stuffing anger makes me sick.
I allow myself freedom with all my emotions, including anger.

I've never been angry.
Healthy expressions of anger keep me healthy.

My neighbors are so noisy.
I release the need to be disturbed.

Nobody asks me what I think.
My opinions are valued.

"I give myself permission to acknowledge my feelings."

Peaceful-Living Treatment

I am one with Life, and all of Life loves and supports me. Therefore, I claim for myself love and acceptance on all levels. I accept all of my emotions and can express them appropriately when the occasion arises. I am not my parents, nor am I attached to their patterns of anger and judgment. I have learned to observe rather than react, and now life is much less tumultuous. I am my own unique self, and I no longer choose to sweat the small stuff. I have peace of mind. This is the truth of my being, and I accept it as so. All is well in my inner being.

CHAPTER 6

Affirmations for Addictions

"No person, place, or thing has any power over me. I am free."

Addictions Checklist

Check the items below that you believe are applicable to you. By the end of this chapter, you'll be able to counter these negative thoughts with positive ones.

- ❏ I want to relieve my pain *now*.
- ❏ Smoking cigarettes reduces my stress.
- ❏ Having lots of sex keeps me from thinking.
- ❏ I can't stop eating.
- ❏ Drinking makes me popular.
- ❏ I need perfection.
- ❏ I gamble too much.
- ❏ I need my tranquilizers.
- ❏ I can't stop buying things.
- ❏ I have a problem getting away from abusive relationships.

Addictive behavior is another way of saying "I'm not good enough." When we're caught in this type of behavior, we're trying to run away from ourselves. We don't want to be in touch with our feelings. Something that we're believing, remembering, saying, or doing is too painful for us to look at; so we overeat, drink, engage in compulsive sexual behavior, take pills, spend money that we don't have, and attract abusive love relationships.

There are 12-step programs that deal with most of these addictions, and they work well for thousands of people. If you have a serious addiction problem, I encourage you to attend Alcoholics Anonymous (AA) or Al-Anon meetings. They will provide you with the help you need as you go through these important changes.

In this chapter, we can't hope to duplicate the results that these programs have produced for people with addictive behavior. I believe that we must first realize that there's a need in ourselves for these compulsive actions. That need must be released before the behavior can be changed.

Loving and approving of yourself, trusting in the process of life, and feeling safe because you know the power of your own mind are extremely important issues when dealing with addictive behaviors. My experience with addicted persons has shown me that most of these individuals possess a deep self-hatred. They're very unforgiving of themselves. Day after day, they punish themselves. Why? Because somewhere along the line (most likely when they were children), they bought into the idea that they weren't good enough—they were "bad" and in need of punishment.

Early childhood experiences that involve physical, emotional, or sexual abuse contribute to that type of self-hatred. Honesty, forgiveness, self-love, and a willingness to live in the truth can help heal these early wounds and give addictive individuals a reprieve from their behavior. I also find the addictive personality to be a fearful one. There's a great fear of letting go and trusting the process of life. As long as we believe that the world is an unsafe place with people and situations waiting to "get" us—then that belief will be our reality.

Are you willing to let go of ideas and beliefs that don't support and nurture you? If so, then you're ready to continue this journey.

EXERCISE: Release Your Addictions

This is where the changes take place—right here and now in your own mind! Take some deep breaths; close your eyes; and think about the person, place, or thing that you're addicted to. Think of the insanity behind the addiction. You're trying to fix what you think is wrong inside of you by grabbing on to something that's outside of you. The point of power is in the present moment, and you can begin to make a shift today.

Once again, be willing to release the need. Say: *"I am willing to release the need for _____ in my life. I release it now and trust in the process of life to meet my needs."*

Say this statement every morning in your daily meditation and prayers. You've taken another step toward freedom.

EXERCISE: Your Secret Addiction

List ten secrets you've never shared with anyone regarding your addiction. If you're an overeater, maybe you've eaten out of a garbage can. If you're an alcoholic, you may have kept alcohol in your car so you could drink while driving. If you're a compulsive gambler, perhaps you put your family in jeopardy in order to borrow money to feed your gambling problem. Be totally honest and open.

How do you feel now? Look at your "worst" secret. Visualize yourself at that period in your life, and *love* that person. Express how much you love and forgive him or her. Look into the mirror and say: "I forgive you, and I love you exactly as you are." Breathe.

EXERCISE: Ask Your Family

Let's go back to your childhood for a moment and answer a few questions.

1. My mother always made me . . .
2. What I really wanted her to say was . . .
3. What my mother really didn't know was . . .
4. My father told me I shouldn't . . .
5. If my father only knew . . .
6. I wish I could have told my father . . .
7. Mother, I forgive you for . . .
8. Father, I forgive you for . . .

Many people tell me that they can't enjoy today because of something that happened in the past. Holding on to the past *only hurts us*. We're refusing to live in the moment. The past is over and can't be changed. This is the only moment we can experience.

EXERCISE: Releasing the Past

Now let's clean up the past in your mind. Release the emotional attachment to it. Allow the memories to just be memories.

If you remember what you wore at the age of ten, there's usually no attachment. It's just a memory. That can be the same for *all* of the past events in our lives. As you let go, you become free to use all of your mental power to enjoy this moment and create a bright future.

You don't have to keep punishing ourselves for the past.

1. List all of the things you're willing to let go of.
2. How willing are you to let go? Notice your reactions, and write them down.
3. What will you have to do to let these things go? How willing are you to do so?

EXERCISE: Self-Approval

Since self-hatred plays such an important role in addictive behavior, we will now do one of my favorite exercises. I've given this exercise to thousands of people, and the results are phenomenal.

Every time you think about your addiction for the next month, say over and over to yourself, *"I approve of myself."*

Do this three or four hundred times a day. No, it's not too many times. When you're worrying, you'll go over your problem at least that many times in a day. Let "I approve of myself" become a waking mantra, something that you say over and over to yourself, almost nonstop.

Saying this statement is guaranteed to bring up everything in your consciousness that is in opposition. When a negative thought comes into your mind, such as "How can you approve of yourself—you spent all of your money," or "You just ate two pieces of cake," or "You'll never amount to anything"—or whatever your negative babble may be—*this* is the time to take mental control. Give this thought no importance. Just see it for what it is—another way to keep you stuck in the past. Gently say to this thought, "Thank you for sharing. I let you go. I approve of myself." These thoughts of resistance will have no power over you unless you choose to believe them.

The statements in the checklist at the beginning of this chapter are repeated below, along with an affirmation corresponding to each belief. Make these affirmations part of your daily routine. Say them often in the car, at work, while looking in the mirror, or anytime you feel your negative beliefs surfacing.

I want to relieve my pain *now.*
I am at peace.

Smoking cigarettes reduces my stress.
I release my stress with deep breathing.

Having lots of sex keeps me from thinking.
I have the power, strength, and knowledge to handle
everything in my life.

I can't stop eating.
I nourish myself with my own love.

Drinking makes me popular.
I radiate acceptance, and I am deeply loved by others.

I need perfection.
I release that silly belief. I am enough just as I am.

I gamble too much.
I am open to the wisdom within. I am at peace.

I need my tranquilizers.
I relax into the flow of Life and let Life provide all that I need
easily and comfortably.

I can't stop buying things.
I am willing to create new thoughts about myself and my life.

I have a problem getting away from abusive relationships.
No one can mistreat me. I love, appreciate, and respect myself.

"I give myself permission to change."

A Healing Treatment for Addictions

I am one with Life, and all of Life loves me and supports me. Therefore, I claim for myself high self-worth and self-esteem. I love and appreciate myself on every level. I am not my parents, nor any addictive pattern they may have had. No matter what my past may have been, now in this moment I choose to eliminate all negative self-talk and to love and approve of myself. I am my own unique self, and I rejoice in who I am. I am acceptable and lovable. This is the truth of my being, and I accept it as so. All is well in my world.

CHAPTER 7

Affirmations for Forgiveness

"I am forgiven, and I am free."

Forgiveness Checklist

Check the items below that you believe are applicable to you. By the end of this chapter, you'll be able to counter these negative thoughts with positive ones.

- ❏ I'll never forgive them.
- ❏ What they did was unforgivable.
- ❏ They ruined my life.
- ❏ They did it on purpose.
- ❏ I was so little, and they hurt me so much.
- ❏ They have to apologize first.
- ❏ My resentment keeps me safe.
- ❏ Only weak people forgive.
- ❏ I'm right and they're wrong.
- ❏ It's all my parents' fault.
- ❏ I don't have to forgive anyone.

Do you resonate to several of these statements? Forgiveness is a difficult area for so many people.

We all need to do forgiveness work. Anyone who has a problem with loving themselves is stuck in this area. Forgiveness opens our hearts to self-love. Many of us carry grudges for years and years. We feel self-righteous because of what *they* did to us. I call this being stuck in the prison of self-righteous resentment. We get to be right. We never get to be happy.

I can almost hear you saying, "But you don't know what they did to me; it's unforgivable." Being unwilling to forgive is a terrible thing to do to yourself. Bitterness is like swallowing a teaspoon of poison every day. It accumulates and harms you. It's impossible to be healthy and free when you keep yourself bound to the past. The incident is long gone and over with. Yes, it's true that *they* didn't behave well. However, it's over. You might feel that if you forgive them, then you're saying that what they did to you was okay.

One of our biggest spiritual lessons is to understand that everyone is doing the best they can at any given moment. People can only do so much with the understanding, awareness, and knowledge that they have. Invariably, anyone who mistreats someone was mistreated themselves as a child. The greater the violence, the greater their own inner pain, and the more they may lash out. This is not to say that their behavior is acceptable or excusable. However, for our own spiritual growth, we must be aware of their pain.

The incident is over. Perhaps long over. Let it go. Allow yourself to be free. Come out of prison, and step into the sunshine of life. If the incident is still going on, then ask yourself why you think so little of yourself that you still put up with it. Why do you stay in such a situation? Don't waste time trying to "get even." It doesn't work. What you give out always comes back to you. So drop the past and work on loving yourself in the *now*. Then you'll have a wonderful future.

That person who is the hardest to forgive is the one who can teach you the greatest lessons. When you love yourself enough to rise above the old situation, then understanding and forgiveness will be easy. And you'll be free. Does freedom frighten you? Does it feel safer to be stuck in your old resentment and bitterness?

Mirror Work

It's time to go back to the mirror. Look into your eyes and say with feeling, *"I am willing to forgive!"* Repeat this several times.

What are you feeling? Do you feel stubborn and stuck, or do you feel open and willing?

Just notice your feelings. Don't judge them. Breathe deeply a few times, and repeat the process. Does it feel any different?

EXERCISE: Family Attitudes

1. Was your mother a forgiving person?
2. Was your father?
3. Was bitterness a way of handling hurtful situations in your family?

4. How did your mother get even?

5. What about your father?

6. How do you get even?

7. Do you feel good when you get revenge?

8. Why do you feel this way?

An interesting phenomenon is that when you do your own forgiveness work, other people often respond to it. It's not necessary to go to the persons involved and tell them you forgive them. Sometimes you'll want to do this, but you don't have to. The major work in forgiveness is done in your own heart.

Forgiveness is seldom for "them." It's for us. The person you need to forgive may even be dead.

I've heard from many people who have truly forgiven someone, and then a month or two later, they may receive a phone call or a letter from the other person, asking to be forgiven. This seems to be particularly true when forgiveness exercises are done in front of a mirror, so as you do this exercise, notice how deep your feelings might be.

Mirror Work

Mirror work is often uncomfortable and something you may want to avoid. If you're standing in the bathroom doing mirror work, it's far too easy to run out the door. I believe that you receive the most benefits if you sit in front of a mirror. I like to use the big dressing mirror on the back of my bedroom door. I settle in with a box of tissues.

Give yourself time to do this exercise, or you can do it over and over. Most likely you have lots of people to forgive.

Sit in front of your mirror. Close your eyes, and breathe deeply several times. Think of the many people who have hurt you in your life. Let them pass through your mind. Now open your eyes and begin talking to one of them.

Say something like: "You've hurt me deeply. However, I won't stay stuck in the past any longer. I am willing to forgive you." Take a breath and then say, "I forgive you, and I set you free." Breathe again and say, "You are free, and I am free."

Notice how you feel. You may feel resistance, or you may feel clear. If you feel resistance, just breathe and say, "I am willing to release all resistance."

This may be a day when you can forgive several people. It may be a day when you can forgive only one. It doesn't matter. No matter how you're doing this exercise, it's perfect for you. Forgiveness can be like peeling away the layers of an onion. If there are too many layers, put the onion away for a day. You can always come back and peel another layer. Acknowledge yourself for being willing to even begin this exercise.

As you continue to do this exercise, today or another day, expand your list of those to forgive. Remember:

- family members
- teachers
- kids at school
- lovers
- friends
- co-workers
- government agencies or figures
- church members or personnel
- medical professionals
- God
- other authority figures
- yourself

Most of all, forgive yourself. Stop being so hard on yourself. Self-punishment isn't necessary. You were doing the very best you could.

Sit in front of the mirror once again with your list. Say to each person on your list, "I forgive you for _____." Breathe. "I forgive you, and I set you free."

Continue to go down your list. If you feel that you're no longer angry or resentful toward someone, cross them off. If you're not free of anger, put them aside and come back to the work later.

As you continue to do this exercise, you'll find burdens melting off your shoulders. You may be surprised by the amount of old baggage you've been carrying. Be gentle with yourself as you go through the cleansing process.

EXERCISE: Make a List

Put on some soft music—something that will make you feel relaxed and peaceful. Now take a pad and pen and let your mind drift. Go back into the past, and think of all the things that you're angry with yourself about. Write them down. Write them *all* down. You may discover that you've never forgiven yourself for the humiliation of wetting your pants in the first grade. What a long time to carry *that* burden!

Sometimes it's easier to forgive others than to forgive ourselves. We're often hard on ourselves and demand perfection. Any mistakes we make are severely punished. It's time to go beyond that old attitude.

Mistakes are the way you learn. If you were perfect, there wouldn't be anything to learn. You wouldn't need to be on the planet. Being "perfect" will not get your parents' love and approval—it will only make you feel "wrong" and not good enough. Lighten up and stop treating yourself that way.

Forgive yourself. Let it go. Give yourself the space to be spontaneous and free. There's no need for shame and guilt.

Go outside to a beach, a park, or even an empty lot, and let yourself run. Don't jog. Run wild and free—turn somersaults, skip along the street—and laugh while you're doing it! Take your inner child with you and have some fun. So what if someone sees you? This is for your freedom!

The statements in the checklist at the beginning of this chapter are repeated below, along with an affirmation corresponding to each belief. Make these affirmations part of your daily routine. Say them often in the car, at work, while looking in the mirror, or anytime you feel your negative beliefs surfacing.

I'll never forgive them.
This is a new moment. I am free to let go.

What they did was unforgivable.
I am willing to go beyond my own limitations.

They ruined my life.
I take responsibility for my own life. I am free.

They did it on purpose.
They were doing the best they could with the knowledge, understanding, and awareness that they had at the time.

I was so little, and they hurt me so much.
I am grown up now, and I take loving care of my inner child.

They have to apologize first.
My spiritual growth is not dependent on others.

My resentment keeps me safe.
I release myself from prison. I am safe and free.

Only weak people forgive.
It is empowering to forgive and let go.

I'm right and they're wrong.
There is no right or wrong. I move beyond my judgment.

It's all my parents' fault.
My parents treated me in the way <u>they</u> had been treated.
I forgive them—and their parents, too.

I don't have to forgive anyone.
I refuse to limit myself. I am always willing to take the next step.

"I give myself permission to let go."

Forgiveness Treatment

I am one with Life, and all of Life loves and supports me. Therefore, I claim for myself an open heart filled with love. We are all doing the best we can at any given moment, and this is also true for me. The past is over and done. I am not my parents, nor their own patterns of resentment. I am my own unique self; and I choose to open my heart and allow the love, compassion, and understanding to flush out all memories of past pain. I am free to be all that I can be. This is the truth of my being, and I accept it as so. All is well in my life.

CHAPTER 8

Affirmations for Work

"It is a joy to express my creativity and be appreciated."

Work Checklist

Check the items below that you believe are applicable to you. By the end of this chapter, you'll be able to counter these negative thoughts with positive ones.

- ❏ I hate my job.
- ❏ My job is too stressful.
- ❏ No one appreciates me at work.
- ❏ I always get dead-end jobs.
- ❏ My boss is abusive.
- ❏ Everyone expects too much of me.
- ❏ My co-workers drive me crazy.
- ❏ My job offers no creativity.
- ❏ I'll never be successful.
- ❏ There's no chance for advancement.
- ❏ My job doesn't pay well.

Let's explore our thinking in the work area. Our jobs and the work that we do are a reflection of our own self-worth and our value to the world. On one level, work is an exchange of time and services for money. I like to believe that all forms of business are opportunities for us to bless and prosper each other.

The *kind* of work we do is important to us because we're unique individuals. We want to feel that we're making a contribution to the world. We need to express our own talents, intelligence, and creative ability.

There are problems that can occur in the workplace, though. You may not get along with your boss or your co-workers. You may not feel appreciated or recognized for the work that you do. Promotional opportunities or a specific job may elude you.

Remember that whatever position you may find yourself in . . . your thinking got you there. The people around you are only mirroring what *you* believe you deserve.

Thoughts can be changed, and situations can be changed as well. That boss whom we find intolerable could become our champion. That dead-end position with no hope of advancement may open up to a new career full of possibilities. The co-worker who is so annoying might turn out to be, if not a friend, at least someone who's easier to get along with. The salary that we find insufficient can increase in the twinkle of an eye. We could find a wonderful new job.

There are an infinite number of channels if we can change our thinking. Let's open ourselves up to all the possibilities. We must accept in consciousness that abundance and fulfillment can come from anywhere.

The change may be small at first, such as an additional assignment from your boss in which you could demonstrate your intelligence and creativity. You might find that if you don't treat a co-worker like they're the enemy, a noticeable change in behavior may occur. Whatever the change may be, accept and rejoice in it. You're not alone. You *are* the change. The Power that created you has given *you* the power to create your own experiences!

EXERCISE: Center Yourself

Take a moment to center yourself. Take your right hand and place it over your lower stomach area. Think of this area as the center of your being. Breathe. Look into your mirror again, and say, *"I am willing to release the need to be so unhappy at work."* Say it two more times. Each time, say it in a different way. What you want to do is increase your commitment to change.

EXERCISE: Think about Your Work Life

1. If you could become anything, what would you be?
2. If you could have any job that you wanted, what would it be?
3. What would you like to change about your current job?
4. What would you change about your employer?
5. Do you work in a pleasant environment?
6. Whom do you need to forgive the most at work?

Mirror Work

Sit in front of a mirror. Breathe deeply. Center yourself. Now talk to those individuals at work you're the most angry with. Tell them why you're angry and express how much they've hurt you, threatened you, or violated your space and boundaries. Let everything out—don't hold back! Explain the type of behavior you expect in the future, and forgive them for not being who you wanted them to be.

Take a breath. Ask them to give you respect, and offer the same to them. Affirm that you can both have a harmonious working relationship.

Blessing with Love

Blessing with love is a powerful tool to use in any work environment. Send it ahead of you before you arrive at your place of employment. Bless every person, place, or thing there with love. If you have a problem with a co-worker, a boss, a supplier, or even the temperature in the building, bless it with love. Affirm that you and the person or situation are in agreement and in perfect harmony:

"I am in perfect harmony with my work environment and everyone in it."

"I always work in harmonious surroundings."

"I honor and respect each person, and they, in turn, honor and respect me."

"I bless this situation with love and know that it works out the best for everyone concerned."

"I bless you with love and release you to your highest good."

"I bless this job and release it to someone who will love it, and I am free to accept a wonderful new opportunity."

Select or adapt one of these affirmations to fit a situation in your workplace, and repeat it over and over. Every time a certain person or situation comes to mind, repeat the affirmation. Eliminate the negative energy in your mind. You *can,* just by thinking, change the experience.

EXERCISE: Self-Worth in Your Job

Let's examine your feelings of self-worth in the area of employment. After answering each of the following questions, write an affirmation (in the present tense).

1. **Do I feel worthy of having a good job?**

    Sample Answer: *Sometimes I don't feel good enough.*
    Sample Affirmation: *I am totally adequate for all situations.*

2. **What do I fear most about work?**

    Sample Answer: *My employer will find out that I'm no good, will fire me, and I won't find another job.*
    Sample Affirmation: *I center myself in safety and accept the perfection of my life. All is well.*

3. **What am I "getting" from this belief?**

Sample Answer: *I people-please at work, and turn my employer into a parent.*
Sample Affirmation: *It is my mind that creates my experiences. I am unlimited in my ability to create the good in my life.*

4. **What do I fear will happen if I let go of this belief?**

Sample Answer: *I would have to grow up and be responsible.*
Sample Affirmation: *I know that I am worthwhile. It is safe for me to succeed. Life loves me.*

Visualization

What would the perfect job be? Take a moment to see yourself in the job. Visualize yourself in the environment, see your co-workers, and feel what it would be like to do work that's completely fulfilling—while you earn a good salary. Hold that vision for yourself, and know that it has been fulfilled in consciousness.

The statements in the checklist at the beginning of this chapter are repeated below, along with an affirmation corresponding to each belief. Make these affirmations part of your daily routine. Say them often in the car, at work, while looking in the mirror, or anytime you feel your negative beliefs surfacing.

I hate my job.
I enjoy the work I do and the people I work with.

My job is too stressful.
I am always relaxed at work.

No one appreciates me at work.
My work is recognized by everyone.

I always get dead-end jobs.
I turn every experience into an opportunity.

My boss is abusive.
All my supervisors treat me with love and respect.

Everyone expects too much of me.
I am capable, competent, and in the perfect place.

My co-workers drive me crazy.
I see the best in everyone, and they respond in kind.

My job offers no creativity.
My thoughts create a wonderful new opportunity.

I'll never be successful.
Everything I touch is a success.

There's no chance for advancement.
New doors are opening all the time.

My job doesn't pay well.
I am open and receptive to new avenues of income.

"I give myself permission to be creatively fulfilled."

Work Treatment

I am one with Life, and all of Life loves and supports me. Therefore, I claim the best creative self-expression possible. My work environment is deeply fulfilling to me. I am loved, appreciated, and respected. I am not my parents, nor do I duplicate their own work-experience patterns. I am my own unique self, and I choose to do work that brings me even more satisfaction than the money. Work is now a joy for me. This is the truth of my being, and I accept it as so. All is well in my working world.

CHAPTER 9

Affirmations for Money and Prosperity

"Infinite prosperity is mine to share; I am blessed."

Money and Prosperity Checklist

Check the items below that you believe are applicable to you. By the end of this chapter, you'll be able to counter these negative thoughts with positive ones.

- ❏ I can't save money.
- ❏ I don't earn enough.
- ❏ My credit rating is bad.
- ❏ Money slips through my fingers.
- ❏ Everything is so expensive.
- ❏ Why does everyone else have money?
- ❏ I can't pay my bills.
- ❏ Bankruptcy is around the corner.
- ❏ I can't save for retirement.
- ❏ I can't let go of money.

What are your beliefs about money? Do you believe that there is enough? Do you attach your self-worth to it? Do you think that it will bring you your heart's desire? Are you friends with money, or is it an enemy?

Having more money is not enough. We need to learn how to *deserve* and *enjoy* the money we have.

Large amounts of money is not a guarantee of prosperity. People who have a lot of money can still be engulfed in poverty consciousness. They can be more fearful about not having money than a homeless person who lives on the street. The ability to enjoy their money and to live in a world of abundance may elude them. Socrates, the great philosopher, once said that "contentment is natural wealth; luxury is artificial poverty."

As I've said many times, your prosperity consciousness is not dependent upon money; your flow of money is dependent upon your prosperity consciousness.

Our pursuit of money *must* contribute to the quality of our lives. If it doesn't—that is, if we hate what we do in order to make money, then money will be useless. Prosperity involves the *quality* of our lives, as well as any amount of money that we possess.

Prosperity is not defined by money alone; it encompasses time, love, success, joy, comfort, beauty, and wisdom. For example, you can be poor with respect to time. If you feel rushed, pressured, and harried, then your time is steeped in poverty. But if you feel you have all the time you need to finish any task at hand, and you're confident that you can finish any job, then you're prosperous when it comes to time.

Or what about success? Do you feel that it's beyond your reach and completely unattainable? Or do you feel that you can be a success in your own right? If you do, then you're rich with respect to success.

Know that whatever your beliefs are, they can be changed in *this* moment. The power that created you has given *you* the power to create your own experiences. You can change!

Mirror Work

Stand up with your arms outstretched, and say, *"I am open and receptive to all good."* How does that feel?

Now, look into the mirror and say it again with feeling.

What kinds of emotions come up for you? It feels liberating, doesn't it? Do this exercise every morning. It's a wonderfully symbolic gesture that may increase your prosperity consciousness and bring more good into your life.

EXERCISE: Your Feelings about Money

Let's examine your feelings of self-worth in this area. Answer the following questions as best you can.

1. Go back to the mirror. Look into your eyes and say, "My biggest fear about money is _____."
   Write down your answer and tell why you feel that way.

2. What did you learn about money as a child?

3. Did your parents grow up during the Depression? What were their thoughts about money?

4. How were finances handled in your family?

5. How do you handle money now?

6. What would you like to change about your money consciousness?

EXERCISE: Your Money Consciousness

Let's further examine your feelings of self-worth in the money area. Answer the following questions as best you can. After each negative belief, create a positive affirmation in the present tense to take its place.

1. **Do I feel worthy of having and enjoying money?**

   Sample Answer: *Not really. I get rid of money as soon as I get it.*
   Sample Affirmation: *I bless the money I have. It is safe to save money and let my money work for me.*

2.   **What is my greatest fear regarding money?**

Sample Answer: *I'm afraid that I'll always be broke.*
Sample Affirmation: *I now accept limitless abundance from a limitless Universe.*

3.   **What am I "getting" from this belief?**

Sample Answer: *I get to stay poor, and I get to be taken care of by others.*
Sample Affirmation: *I claim my own power and lovingly create my own reality. I trust the process of life.*

4.   **What do I fear will happen to me if I let go of this belief?**

Sample Answer: *No one will love me and take care of me.*
Sample Affirmation: *I am safe in the Universe, and all life loves and supports me.*

EXERCISE: Your Use of Money

Write down three ways in which you're critical of your use of money. Maybe you're constantly in debt, you can't save money, or you can't enjoy your money.

Think of one example in each of these instances where you *haven't* acted out the undesirable behavior.

Example:

I criticize myself for: *compulsively spending money and being in constant debt. I can't seem to hold down my spending.*

I praise myself for: *paying the rent today. It's the first of the month, and I am making my payment on time.*

Visualizations

Place your hand over your heart, take a few deep breaths, and relax. See yourself acting out your worst scenario with money. Perhaps you borrowed money that you couldn't return, bought something you knew you couldn't afford, or declared bankruptcy. See yourself acting out the behavior—*love that person that you were.* Know that you were doing the very best you could with the knowledge, understanding, and capability that you had. *Love that person.* See yourself acting out behavior that might embarrass you today, and *love that person.*

What would it be like to have all the things you've always wanted? What would they look like? Where would you go? What would you do? Feel it. Enjoy it. Be creative and *have fun.*

The statements in the checklist at the beginning of this chapter are repeated below, along with an affirmation corresponding to each belief. Make these affirmations part of your daily routine. Say them often in the car, at work, while looking in the mirror, or anytime you feel your negative beliefs surfacing.

I can't save money.
I am worthy of having money in the bank.

I don't earn enough.
My income is constantly increasing.

My credit rating is bad.
My credit rating is getting better all the time.

Money slips through my fingers.
I spend money wisely.

Everything is so expensive.
I always have as much as I need.

Why does everyone else have money?
I have as much money as I can accept.

I can't pay my bills.
I bless all of my bills with love. I pay them on time.

Bankruptcy is around the corner.
I am always financially solvent.

I can't save for retirement.
I am joyfully providing for my retirement.

I can't let go of money.
I enjoy saving, and I spend in balance.

"I give myself permission to prosper."

Money and Prosperity Treatment

I am one with Life, and all of Life loves and supports me. Therefore, I claim for myself an abundant share of the prosperity of life. I have an abundance of time, love, joy, comfort, beauty, wisdom, success, and money. I am not my parents, nor their own financial patterns. I am my own unique self, and I choose to be open and receptive to prosperity in all its many forms. I am deeply grateful to Life for all its generosity to me. My income constantly increases, and I continue to prosper for the rest of my life. This is the truth of my being, and I accept it as so. All is well in my prosperous world.

CHAPTER 10

Affirmations for Friends

"I am a friend to myself."

Friendship Checklist

Check the items below that you believe are applicable to you. By the end of this chapter, you'll be able to counter these negative thoughts with positive ones.

- ❏ My friends don't support me.
- ❏ Everyone is so judgmental.
- ❏ Nobody sees it my way.
- ❏ My boundaries are not respected.
- ❏ I can't keep friends for too long.
- ❏ I can't let my friends really know me.
- ❏ I give my friends advice for their own good.
- ❏ I don't know how to be a friend.
- ❏ I don't know how to ask for help from my friends.
- ❏ I don't know how to say no to a friend.

Friendships can be our most enduring and important relationships. We can live without lovers or spouses. We can live without our primary families. But most of us cannot live happily without friends. I believe that we choose our parents before we're born into this planet, but we choose our friends on a more conscious level.

Ralph Waldo Emerson, the great American philosopher and writer, wrote an essay on friendship, calling it the "nectar of God." He explained that in romantic relationships, one person is always trying to change the other, but friends can stand back and look at one another with appreciation and respect.

Friends can be an extension or a substitute for the nuclear family. There's a great need in most of us to share life experiences with others. Not only do we learn more about others when we engage in friendship, but we can also learn more about ourselves. These relationships are mirrors of our self-worth and self-esteem. They afford us the perfect opportunity to look at ourselves, and the areas where we might need to grow.

When the bond between friends becomes strained, we can look to the negative messages of childhood. It may be time for mental housecleaning. Cleaning the mental house after a lifetime of negative messages is a bit like starting a sound nutritional program after a lifetime of eating junk foods. As you change your diet, your body will throw off a toxic residue, and you may feel worse for a day or two.

So it is when you make a decision to change your mental thought patterns. Your circumstances may worsen for a while, but remember—you may have to dig through a lot of dry weed to get to the rich soil below. But you can do it! I know you can!

EXERCISE: Your Friendships

Write down the following affirmation three times, then answer the questions that follow.

"I am willing to release any pattern within me that creates troubled friendships."

1. What were your first childhood friendships like?
2. How are your friendships today like those childhood friendships?
3. What did you learn about friendship from your parents?
4. What kinds of friends did your parents have?
5. What kinds of friends would you like to have in the future? Be specific.

EXERCISE: Self-Worth and Friendship

Let's examine your self-worth in the area of friendship. Answer each of the following questions below. Then, write a positive affirmation (in the present tense) to replace the old belief.

1. Do I feel worthy of having good friends?

Sample Answer: *No. Why would anyone want to be around me?*
Sample Affirmation: *I love and accept myself, and I am a magnet for friends.*

2. **What do I fear most about having close friends?**

   Sample Answer: *I am afraid of betrayal. I don't feel that I can trust anyone.*
   Sample Affirmation: *I trust myself, I trust life, and I trust my friends.*

3. **What am I "getting" from this belief?**

   Sample Answer: *I get to be judgmental. I wait for my friends to make one false move so that I can show them that they're wrong.*
   Sample Affirmation: *All of my friendships are successful. I am a loving and nurturing friend.*

4. **What do I fear will happen if I let go of this belief?**

   Sample Answer: *I'll lose control. I'd have to let people really get to know me.*
   Sample Affirmation: *Loving others is easy when I love and accept myself.*

If we're all responsible for the events in our lives, then there's no one to blame. Whatever is happening "out there" is only a reflection of our own inner thinking.

EXERCISE: Thinking about Your Friends

Think of three events in your life where you feel you were mistreated or abused by friends. Perhaps a friend betrayed a confidence or abandoned you in a time of need. Maybe this person interfered with a spouse or mate.

In each case, name the event, and write down the thoughts you had at the time that preceded each event.

Sample Event: *When I was 16 years old, my best friend Susie turned on me and started to spread vicious rumors. When I tried to confront her, she lied to me. I was friendless my entire senior year.*

Sample Thoughts: *I did not deserve friends. I was drawn to my friend Susie because she was cold and judgmental. I was used to being judged and criticized.*

EXERCISE: The Support of Your Friends

Now, think of three times in your life when you were supported by friends. Perhaps a good friend stood up for you or gave you money when you needed it. Maybe this person helped you resolve a difficult situation.

In each case, name the event, and write down the thoughts you had at the time that preceded each event.

Sample Event: *I'll always remember Helen. When people at my first job were making fun of me because I said something stupid at a meeting, Helen stood up for me. She helped me through my embarrassment and saved my job.*

My Deepest Thoughts Were: *Even if I make a mistake, someone will always help me. I deserve to be supported. Women support me.*

Visualizations

Which friends do you need to acknowledge? Take a moment to visualize them. Look those people in the eye and say: "I thank you and bless you with love for being there for me when I needed you. May your life be filled with joy."

Which friends do you need to forgive? Take a moment to visualize them. Look at those people in the eye and say: "I forgive you for not acting the way I wanted you to. I forgive you and I set you free."

The statements in the checklist at the beginning of this chapter are repeated below, along with an affirmation corresponding to each belief. Make these affirmations part of your daily routine. Say them often in the car, at work, while looking in the mirror, or anytime you feel your negative beliefs surfacing.

My friends don't support me.
My friends are loving and supportive.

Everyone is so judgmental.
As I release all criticism, judgmental people leave my life.

Nobody sees it my way.
I am open and receptive to all points of view.

My boundaries are not respected.
I respect others, and they respect me.

I can't keep friends for too long.
My love and acceptance of others creates lasting friendships.

I can't let my friends really know me.
It is safe for me to be open.

I give my friends advice for their own good.
I leave my friends alone. We both have total freedom to be ourselves.

I don't know how to be a friend.
I trust my inner wisdom to guide me.

I don't know how to ask for help from my friends.
It is safe for me to ask for what I want.

I don't know how to say no to a friend.
I move beyond those limitations and express myself honestly.

"I give myself permission to be a friend."

Friendship Treatment

I am one with Life, and all of Life loves and supports me. Therefore, I claim for myself a joyous, loving circle of friends. We all have such good times individually and together. I am not my parents nor their relationships. I am my own unique self; and I choose to only allow supportive, nurturing people in my world. Wherever I go I am greeted with warmth and friendliness. I deserve the best friends, and I allow my life to be filled with love and joy. This is the truth of my being, and I accept it as so. All is well in my friendly world.

CHAPTER 11

Affirmations for Love and Intimacy

"Love surrounds me. I am loving, lovable, and loved."

Love and Intimacy Checklist

Check the items below that you believe are applicable to you. By the end of this chapter, you'll be able to counter these negative thoughts with positive ones.

- ❏ I'm afraid of rejection.
- ❏ Love never lasts.
- ❏ I feel trapped.
- ❏ Love scares me.
- ❏ I have to do everything *their* way.
- ❏ If I take care of myself, they'll leave me.
- ❏ I'm jealous.
- ❏ I can't be myself.
- ❏ I'm not good enough.
- ❏ I don't want a marriage like my parents had.
- ❏ I don't know how to love.

❏ I'll get hurt.
❏ I can't say no to someone I love.
❏ Everybody leaves me.

How did you experience love as a child? Did you observe your parents expressing love and affection? Were you raised with lots of hugs? Or in your family, was love expressed through fighting, yelling, crying, door-slamming, manipulation, control, silence, or revenge? If it was, then you'll most likely seek out similar experiences as an adult. You'll find people who will reinforce those ideas. If, as a child, you looked for love and found pain, then as an adult, you'll find pain instead of love . . . unless you release your old family patterns.

EXERCISE: Your Feelings about Love

Answer the following questions as best you can.

1. How did your last relationship end?

2. How did the one before that end?

3. Think about your last two intimate relationships. What were the major issues between you?

4. How did these issues remind you of your relationship with one or both of your parents?

Perhaps all of your relationships ended as a result of your partner leaving you. The need in you to be left could stem from a divorce, a parent withdrawing from you because you weren't what they wanted you to be, or a death in the family.

To change the pattern, you need to forgive your parent *and* understand that you don't have to repeat this old behavior. You free them, and you free yourself.

For every habit or pattern we repeat over and over again, there's a *need within us* for such repetition. The need corresponds to some belief that we have. If there was no need, we would not have to have it, do it, or be it. Self-criticism does not break the pattern—letting go of the need does.

Mirror Work

Using your mirror, look into your eyes, breathe, and say: "I am willing to release the need for relationships that don't nourish and support me." Say this five times in the mirror; each time you say it, give it more meaning. Think of some of your relationships as you say it.

EXERCISE: Your Relationships

Answer the following questions as best you can.

1. What did you learn about love as a child?
2. Did you ever have a boss who was "just like" one of your parents? How?
3. Is your partner/spouse like one of your parents? How?
4. What or whom would you have to forgive in order to change this pattern?
5. From your new understanding, what would you like your relationship to be like?

Your old thoughts and beliefs continue to form your experiences until you let them go. Your future thoughts haven't been formed, and you don't know what they'll be. Your current thought, the one you're thinking right now, is totally under your control.

We are the only ones who choose our thoughts. We may habitually think the same thought over and over so that it doesn't seem as if we're choosing it. But we did make the original choice. However, we *can* refuse to think certain thoughts. How often have you refused to think a *positive* thought about yourself? Well, you can also refuse to think a *negative* thought about yourself. It just takes practice.

EXERCISE: Love and Intimacy

Let's examine these beliefs. Answer each of the questions below, then write a positive affirmation (in the present tense) to replace the old belief.

1. **Do I feel worthy of having an intimate relationship?**

    Sample Answer: *No. Another person would run if they really knew me.*
    Sample Affirmation: *I am lovable and worth knowing.*

2. **Am I afraid to love?**

    Sample Answer: *Yes. I'm afraid that my mate won't be faithful.*
    Sample Affirmation: *I am always secure in love.*

3. **What am I "getting" from this belief?**

    Sample Answer: *I don't let romance into my life.*
    Sample Affirmation: *It is safe for me to open my heart to let love in.*

4. **What do I fear will happen if I let go of this belief?**

    Sample Answer: *I'll be taken advantage of and be hurt.*
    Sample Affirmation: *It is safe for me to share my innermost self with others.*

The statements in the checklist at the beginning of this chapter are repeated below, along with an affirmation corresponding to each belief. Make these affirmations part of your daily routine. Say them often in the car, at work, while looking in the mirror, or anytime you feel your negative beliefs surfacing.

I'm afraid of rejection.
I love and accept myself, and I am safe.

Love never lasts.
Love is eternal.

I feel trapped.
Love makes me feel free.

Love scares me.
It is safe for me to be in love.

I have to do everything *their* way.
We are always equal partners.

If I take care of myself, they'll leave me.
We each take care of ourselves.

I'm jealous.
Jealousy is only insecurity. I now develop my own self-esteem.

I can't be myself.
People love me when I am myself.

I'm not good enough.
I am worthy of love.

I don't want a marriage like my parents had.
I am not my parents. I go beyond their patterns.

I don't know how to love.
Loving myself and others gets easier every day.

I'll get hurt.
The more I open up to love, the safer I am.

I can't say no to someone I love.
My partner and I respect each other's decisions.

Everybody leaves me.
I now create a long-lasting, loving relationship.

"I give myself permission to experience intimate love."

Love and Intimacy Treatment

I am one with Life, and all of Life loves and supports me. Therefore, I claim love and intimacy in my world. I am worthy of love. I am not my parents, nor their own relationship patterns. I am my own unique self, and I choose to create and keep a long-lasting, loving relationship—one that nurtures and supports us both in every way. We have great compatibility and similar rhythms, and we bring out the best in each other. We're romantic, and we're the best of friends. I rejoice in this long-term relationship. This is the truth of my being, and I accept it as so. All is well in my loving world.

CHAPTER 12

Affirmations for Aging

"I am beautiful and empowered at every age."

Aging Checklist

Check the items below that you believe are applicable to you. By the end of this chapter, you'll be able to counter these negative thoughts with positive ones.

- ❏ I'm afraid of getting old.
- ❏ I'm scared I'll get wrinkled and fat.
- ❏ I don't want to end up in a nursing home.
- ❏ Being old means I'll be ugly and unwanted.
- ❏ Being old means being sick.
- ❏ No one wants to be around an old person.

No matter what age we are, we will all grow older. We will also have great control over *how* we shall age.

What are the things that age us? Certain beliefs about aging, such as the belief that we have to get sick when we get old. The belief in dis-ease. Hating the body. Believing in a lack of time. Anger and hatred. Self-hatred. Bitterness. Shame and guilt. Fear. Prejudice. Self-righteousness. Being judgmental. Carrying burdens. Giving up our control to others. These are all beliefs that age us.

What do you personally believe about aging? Do you look around at the frail and ill and assume that you'll be that way, too? Do you see poverty among the aging and think that that's your destiny as well? Do you notice how lonely many older people are and wonder if you will be in the same position?

We don't have to accept these negative concepts. We can turn all of this around. It doesn't have to continue to be this way. We can take our power back.

Feeling vital and energetic is much more important than a facial line or two (or even more), yet we've agreed that unless we're young and beautiful, we're not acceptable. Why would we agree to such a belief? Where did we lose our love and compassion for ourselves and for each other? We've made living in our bodies an uncomfortable experience. Each day we look for something that's wrong with us, and we worry about every wrinkle. This only makes us feel bad and creates *more* wrinkles. This isn't self-love. This is self-hatred, and it only contributes to our lack of self-esteem.

What are you teaching your children about aging? What is the example you're giving them? Do they see a dynamic, loving person, enjoying each day and looking forward to the future? Or are you a bitter, frightened person, dreading your elder years and expecting to be sick and alone? *Our children learn from us!* And so do our grandchildren. What kind of elder years do we want to help them envision and create?

We used to live very short lives—first only till our mid-teens, then our 20s, then our 30s, then our 40s. Even at the turn of the century, it was considered old to be 50. In 1900, our life expectancy was 47 years. Now we're accepting 80 as a normal life span. Why can't we take a quantum leap in consciousness and make the new level of acceptance 120 or 150 years?!

It's not out of our reach. I see living much longer becoming normal and natural for most of us in a generation or two. Forty-five used to be middle-aged, but that won't be true anymore. I see 75 becoming the new middle age (I'm now in my 84th year). For generations, we've allowed the numbers that correspond to how many years we've been on the planet tell us how to feel and how to behave. As with any other aspect of life, what we mentally accept and believe about aging becomes true for us. Well, it's time to change our beliefs about aging! When I look around and see frail, sick, frightened older people, I say to myself, "It doesn't have to be that way." Many of us have learned that by changing our thinking, we can change our lives.

I know we can change our beliefs about aging and make the aging process a positive, vibrant, healthy experience.

We can change our belief systems. But in order to do so, we "Elders of Excellence" need to *get out of the victim mentality*. As long as we see ourselves as being hapless, powerless individuals; and as long as we depend on the government to "fix" things for us, we'll never progress as a group. However, when we band together and come up with creative solutions for our later years, then we have real power, and we can change our nation and our world for the better.

It's time for our elders to take back their power from the medical and pharmaceutical industries. They're being buffeted about by high-tech medicine, which is very expensive and destroys their health. It's time for all of us (and especially the elders) to learn to take control of our own health. We need to learn about the body-mind connection—to know that what we do, say, and think contributes to either dis-ease or vibrant health.

EXERCISE: Your Beliefs about Aging

Answer the following questions as best you can.

1. How are your parents aging? (Or how *did* they age if they've passed away?)

2. How old do you feel?

3. What are you doing to help our society/country/planet?

4. How do you create love in your life?

5. Who are your positive role models?

6. What are you teaching your children about aging?

7. What are you doing *today* to prepare for healthy, happy, and vital elder years?

8. How do you feel about and treat older people now?

9. How do you envision your life when you're 60, 75, 85?

10. How do you want to be treated when you're older?

11. How do you want to die?

Now go back and mentally turn each negative answer above into a positive affirmation. Envision your later years as your treasure years.

There's a pot of gold at the end of this rainbow. We know the treasures are there. The later years of our life are to be the years of our greatest treasures. We must learn how to make these the best years of our lives. We learn these secrets later in life, and they are to be shared with the generations coming up. I know that what I call "youthening" can be done; it's just a matter of finding out how.

Here are some of the secrets of youthening, as far as I'm concerned:

- Release the word *old* from our vocabulary.
- Turn "aging" into "living longer."
- Be willing to accept new concepts.
- Take a quantum leap in thinking.
- Modify our beliefs.
- Reject manipulation.
- Change what we consider "normal."
- Turn dis-ease into vibrant health.
- Take good care of our bodies.
- Release limiting beliefs.
- Be willing to adapt our thinking.
- Embrace new ideas.
- Accept the truth about ourselves.
- Give selfless service to our communities.

We want to create a conscious ideal of our later years as the most rewarding phase of our lives. We need to know that our future is always bright no matter what our age. We can do this if we just change our thoughts. It's time to dispel the fearful images of old age. It's time to take a quantum leap in our thinking. We need to take the word *old* out of our vocabulary and become a country where the long-lived are still young—and where life expectancy isn't given a finite number. We want to see our *later years* become our *treasure years.*

The statements in the checklist at the beginning of this chapter are repeated below, along with an affirmation corresponding to each belief. Make these affirmations part of your daily routine. Say them often in the car, at work, while looking in the mirror, or anytime you feel your negative beliefs surfacing.

I'm afraid of getting old.
I release all age-related fears.

I'm scared I'll get wrinkled and fat.
I am beautiful in mind and body.

I don't want to end up in a nursing home.
I am self-sufficient and strong.

Being old means I'll be ugly and unwanted.
I love and am loved by everyone in my world.

Being old means being sick.
I have vibrant health no matter what age I am.

No one wants to be around an old person.
People appreciate me at every age.

"I am surrounded by wonderful people throughout my life."

Healthy-Aging Treatment

I am one with Life, and all of Life loves and supports me. Therefore, I claim for myself peace of mind and joy of living for every age of my life. Each day is new and different and brings its own pleasures. I am an active participant in this world. I am an eager student with an intense desire to learn. I take excellent care of my body. I choose thoughts that make me happy. I have a strong spiritual connection that sustains me at all times. I am not my parents, nor do I have to age or die the way they did. I am my own unique self, and I choose to live a deeply fulfilling life until my last day on this planet. I am at peace with living, and I love all of Life. This is the truth of my being, and I accept it as so. All is well in my life.

SOME FINAL THOUGHTS

We've now explored using affirmations in several different areas of life. The previous chapters are merely guidelines to show you the many different ways you can approach creating positive affirmations for yourself.

Put different affirmations in different parts of your home. You might have an affirmation you keep at the office for work issues. If you don't want others to see it, then put it in your desk drawer so only you see it.

A car affirmation for safe and peaceful driving might be on your dashboard. (Hint, hint . . . if you're always cursing at other drivers, then all the poor drivers will automatically be attracted to you. They'll be fulfilling your affirmation.)

Cursing is an affirmation, worrying is an affirmation, and hatred is an affirmation. All of these are attracting to you that which you're affirming. Love, appreciation, gratitude, and compliments are also affirmations and will similarly attract to you that which you're affirming.

This book and meditation program can now send you on the positive pathway to a wonderful life. However, you must use it.

Words sitting in a book will do nothing to improve the quality of your life.

Just as it doesn't matter where you begin cleaning the house, it also doesn't matter which area of your life you begin to change. It's best to start with something simple because you'll get results quickly and therefore develop confidence to tackle the larger issues.

I know you can do it. You'll be so happy about the positive changes that are happening in your life. This will be the start of a new you!

ABOUT THE AUTHOR

Louise Hay, the author of the international bestseller *You Can Heal Your Life,* is a metaphysical lecturer and teacher with more than 50 million books sold worldwide. For more than 30 years, Louise has helped people throughout the world discover and implement the full potential of their own creative powers for personal growth and self-healing. She has appeared on *The Oprah Winfrey Show* and many other TV and radio programs both in the U.S. and abroad.

Websites: **www.LouiseHay.com**® and
www.HealYourLife.com®

BONUS CONTENT

Thank you for purchasing *Experience Your Good Now!* by Louise Hay. This product includes a free download! To access this bonus content, please visit www.hayhouse.com/download and enter the Product ID and Download Codes as they appear below.

**Product ID: 4846
Download Code: ebook**

For further assistance, please contact Hay House Customer Care by phone: US (800) 654-5126 or INTL CC+(760) 431-7695 or visit www.hayhouse.com/contact.php.

Thank you again for your Hay House purchase. Enjoy!

EXPERIENCE YOUR GOOD NOW! Audio Download Track List

1. Intro
2. Meditation for Health
3. Meditation for Forgiveness
4. Meditation for Prosperity
5. Meditation for Creativity
6. Meditation for Relationships
7. Meditation for Job Success
8. Meditation for Stress
9. Meditation for Self-Esteem
10. Conclusion

Caution: This audio program features meditation/visualization exercises that render it inappropriate for use while driving or operating heavy machinery.

Publisher's note: Hay House products are intended to be powerful, inspirational, and life-changing tools for personal growth and healing. They are not intended as a substitute for medical care. Please use this audio program under the supervision of your care provider. Neither the author nor Hay House, Inc., assumes any responsibility for your improper use of this product.

Also by Louise Hay

❤ For Children ❤

The Adventures of Lulu
I Think, I Am! (with Kristina Tracy)
Lulu and the Ant: A Message of Love
Lulu and the Dark: Conquering Fears
Lulu and Willy the Duck: Learning Mirror Work

❤ Audio Programs ❤

Anger Releasing
Cancer
Change and Transition
Dissolving Barriers
Embracing Change
Feeling Fine Affirmations
Forgiveness/Loving the Inner Child
Heal Your Body (audio book)
How to Love Yourself
Life! Reflections on Your Journey (audio book)
Loving Yourself
Meditations for Personal Healing
Meditations to Heal Your Life (audio book)
Morning and Evening Meditations
101 Power Thoughts
Overcoming Fears
The Power Is Within You (audio book)
The Power of Your Spoken Word
Receiving Prosperity
Self-Esteem Affirmations (subliminal)
Self-Healing
Stress-Free Affirmations (subliminal)
Totality of Possibilities
What I Believe/Deep Relaxation
You Can Heal Your Life (audio book)
You Can Heal Your Life Study Course
Your Thoughts Create Your Life

Notes

Notes

Notes

Notes

Notes

Notes

Notes

We hope you enjoyed this Hay House book. If you'd like to receive our online catalog featuring additional information on Hay House books and products, or if you'd like to find out more about the Hay Foundation, please contact:

Hay House, Inc., P.O. Box 5100, Carlsbad, CA 92018-5100
(760) 431-7695 or (800) 654-5126
(760) 431-6948 (fax) or (800) 650-5115 (fax)
www.hayhouse.com® • www.hayfoundation.org

———

Published in Australia by: Hay House Australia Pty. Ltd.,
18/36 Ralph St., Alexandria NSW 2015
Phone: 612-9669-4299 • *Fax:* 612-9669-4144
www.hayhouse.com.au

Published in the United Kingdom by: Hay House UK, Ltd.,
The Sixth Floor, Watson House, 54 Baker Street, London W1U 7BU
Phone: +44 (0)20 3927 7290 • *Fax:* +44 (0)20 3927 7291
www.hayhouse.co.uk

Published in India by: Hay House Publishers India,
Muskaan Complex, Plot No. 3, B-2, Vasant Kunj, New Delhi 110 070
Phone: 91-11-4176-1620 • *Fax:* 91-11-4176-1630
www.hayhouse.co.in

———

<u>Access New Knowledge.</u>
<u>Anytime. Anywhere.</u>

Learn and evolve at your own pace
with the world's leading experts.

www.hayhouseU.com

Printed in the United States
by Baker & Taylor Publisher Services